African Wonder
"Black Harry"
Hoosier

REV. DR. WALTER ARTHUR MCCRAY

Gospelizer

The African Wonder "Black Harry" Hoosier

A Gospelizer of Distinction

REV. DR. WALTER ARTHUR MCCRAY
Gospelizer

— Lessons from His Life, Witness, & Beliefs —

BLACK LIGHT FELLOWSHIP
Chicago, IL

Rev. Dr. Walter Arthur McCray is a *Gospelizer*, a holistic "Good News messenger" of the resurrected Lord, Jesus Christ. He is a seasoned minister, writer, national speaker, and servant of the Church. Rev. Dr. McCray is president of the National Black Evangelical Association, an office held since 1999. He resides with his wife in Chicago.

The African Wonder "Black Harry" Hoosier
A Gospelizer of Distinction

Rev. Dr. Walter Arthur McCray
Gospelizer

Black Light Fellowship
P.O. Box 5369 • Chicago, IL 60680
Phone: 773.826.7790 • Fax: 773.826.7792
Website: www.BlackLightFellowship.com
Email: info@blacklightfellowship.com

Printed in the U.S.A.
16 15 14   1 2 3 4 5

Editorial Services: Mary C. Lewis, MCL Editing, Etc., Chicago, IL
                       http://www.mcleditingetc.com.

ISBN: 978-0-933176-05-8   eBook Edition
ISBN: 978-0-933176-17-1   Paper Edition

Printed on Acid-Free Paper.

To the many

powerful Gospelizers

left under-empowered by the Church.

Contents

The
African Wonder
"Black Harry"
Hoosier

— 1 —

Introduction

Harry Hoosier lived in North Carolina during the colonial period of American history. He was an illiterate circuit rider and a greatly gifted Gospelizer. Popularly known as "The African Wonder" and called "Black Harry," he was a manumitted, African-descended Methodist lay preacher of distinction. Ironically, the Methodist Church never fully empowered him in the ministry. His life of faith and service as a Gospel preacher from humble beginnings who gained renown intrigues the imagination of Black believers especially. His cross-cultural experience and witness beckons investigation that may offer illumination for the ministry of Christ's Church in the 21st century.

I have readily accepted the task of interacting with the life of Harry Hoosier by speaking to the contemporary relevance of his ministry and beliefs as a model of Evangelicalism, especially as this applies to the life and ministry of African-American believers.[1] I am setting this perspective in the context of my publication *Pro-Black, Pro-Christ, Pro-Cross: African-descended Evangelical Identity.*[2] The work wrestles with authentic expressions of Black Evangelical definition along cultural and theological lines. Its message flows within and from the context of African-American Evangelicalism, manifested incipiently in the Church of the Black experience and intentionally in the **National Black Evangelical Association**, organized in 1963. The conversation of *Pro-Black, Pro-Christ, Pro-Cross* occurs in the face of challenges encountered by African-American people and believers, and against the backdrop of white Evangelicalism and manifestations of racism.

— 2 —

A Sketch of Harry Hoosier,
aka Black Harry

First, we should sketch the background and ministry of Harry Hoosier. Though his distinguished preaching is well attested, scholars note the scarcity of complete biographical information on the life of Hoosier,[3] whom some believe is the nick-namesake of Indiana.[4] The following portrait of Hoosier's life emerges from available information.

Black Harry Hoosier was born into slavery in or about 1750 in North Carolina. There is an uncertain record of his conversion.[5] Although Hoosier was illiterate—unable to read a word—as a circuit-riding Methodist lay preacher he was a very effective revivalist.[6] The heritage of our history says ole Black Harry, in 1781, delivered the first Methodist sermon of record by an African-American.[7] A contemporary of Hoosier, Dr. Benjamin Rush (1745-1813), a signer of the Declaration of Independence, noted Black Harry was "the greatest orator in America."[8] Black Harry preached with great power and lived in humility.

As a traveling servant/driver and preacher, Hoosier assisted and gospelized alongside several Methodist bishops: the Rev. Francis Asbury (1745-1815, founder of American Methodism); the Rev. Henry Boehm (1775-1875), the Rev. Richard Whatcoat (1736-1806);

the Rev. Freeborn Garrettson (1752-1827); and the Rev. Thomas Coke (1747-1814), who said of Black Harry, "I really believe he is one of the best preachers in the world."[9]

The itinerant ministry of Black Harry led him into areas of North Carolina, Virginia, Delaware, Maryland, Pennsylvania, New Jersey, New York, and New England. God used the gospelizing of ole Black Harry to draw thousands of Americans, both Black and white, to Christ. According to one scholar, the ministry overlapped the period from 1790 to 1810, when "one-fifth of Methodist membership was comprised of African Americans."[10] Arguably, the ministry of Black Harry contributed substantially to these Black converts, as well as won others who did not choose association with the Methodist church.[11]

Inspired in 1771 by the call of Wesley in England for workers to spread revival in America, Methodist ministers began reaching out to un-churched, poor, common, and marginalized whites and Blacks, especially in the period of the Second Great Awakening (1790s – 1830). Previously manumitted (prior to 1781), the freedman Black Harry was one of the first Blacks to enter into the ministry, which the Methodist Church opened to laypersons. Initially the church leadership limited Black Harry to preach only to those of African descent. However, his gifts of oratory and memorization of hymns and Scripture opened doors for his preaching to both Blacks and whites. At least prior to the institutionalization of the Methodists, the open revival meetings reflected an important aspect of God's kingdom where whites and Blacks comingled to hear from God and fellowship with the church. At times, mixed crowds gathered by the thousands to hear this Black man of God, and especially his sermon on "The Barren Fig Tree," the parable of Jesus recorded in Luke 13:6-9.

Research notes the preaching style of Black Harry. He skillfully modulated his musical voice, spoke with a gifted tongue and exceptional ability for appealing to the heart with a "terrible" persuasiveness, and moved the audience to a "climactic pitch of emotional tension." His hearers knew he could pray a prayer that was "awful, powerful, and overwhelming."[12] Black Harry ministered with passion and zeal. Quakers believed he spoke by "immediate inspiration" from God.[13] Some who heard him were steadfast in attributing his cultural expressions to "Anglo-Saxon" blood, surmising its sure mixture in Black Harry's veins.[14] Perhaps the simplest explanation of Hoosier's delivery and spiritual expressions is the best: This persuasive evangelist brought the cultural Blackness of African-American folk manners to the table of public proclamation of the Gospel.

Much of Black Harry's theological content and preaching would have aligned with his contemporary Methodist ministers. These circuit-riding preachers addressed their message to the poor and marginalized, while emphasizing a personal expression of faith. They preached a ministry of deliverance from sin and the joy of salvation. They exhorted converts to practice holiness in all dimensions of life and to strive for Christian perfection or maturity.[15]

Many Methodist ministers took a stand against slavery, even though they neglected to embrace full racial equality. Some students of history believe the preaching of Black Harry pushed the racial envelope. Covertly he spoke of freedom and justice, and did so to avoid provoking antagonism.[16] In Black Harry's service alongside the outspoken emancipationist Freeborn Garrettson, he suffered for departing from the doctrines of "unconditional election" and "perseverance of the saints," Calvinist beliefs dominant among Protestants at the time.[17] One could expect these prophetic preachers suffered also for the tone of freedom in the Gospel they preached.[18]

Ole Black Harry faced racism and marginalization in the church and society he served. He never received full acceptance as a minister, was never ordained by the Methodist church.[19] Undoubtedly, Black Harry struggled much with the irony of a status falling short of full recognition and respect by the white leadership dominating the church. Perhaps these spiritual, psychological, emotional, and social pressures contributed to Black Harry's season of backsliding. His sin manifested itself in excessive wine drinking, perhaps coupled with unspecified though unfounded accusations of a scandal with a woman named Sally Lyons.[20] He found his life reduced to subsistence as a drunken ragpicker, or street scavenger, in Philadelphia.

Yet, Hoosier the exhorter, as a Black man of God, "kept on comin'." One day he made the steadfast determination that God would deliver his soul from backsliding and addictions. He resolved to encamp beneath a tree to seek the Lord, and made up his mind not to leave that place until the Lord came to his rescue. At that spiritual turning point, Black Harry "got just what he wanted." Through earnest and prevailing prayer, he found the grace of divine help and restoration for his life and ministry. He resumed once again his effectual Gospelizing and finished the course of his ministry to the glory of God.[21]

Black Harry was a man of faith. We have in his own words the affirmative testimony of how he trusted the Lord: "I sing by faith, pray by faith, preach by faith, and do every thing by faith; without faith in the Lord Jesus I can do nothing."[22] The simple and genuine faith of Black Harry that empowered his living in the Gospel ministry is the same faith that rescued the fallen preacher from hopelessly sinking in a sea of personal degeneration and ministerial disqualification.

Having found grace in God to continue his course, the African Wonder went home to be with the Lord in 1806. Both Blacks and whites admired him and accompanied him to his final resting place. They celebrated his fruitful life, and rejoiced in his victory of overcoming the setbacks of his challenging sojourn.

Harry Hoosier fulfilled the call of God in his changing times. Though beset by prejudice and racism as both "insider and an outsider" on the periphery of the church, Black Harry sacrificially persevered as a revivalist in the work of the Lord. In both beliefs and living, he embraced God's kingdom where Christ rules. Black Harry fulfilled the call of God on his life during a time of racial challenges and struggle for change.

— 3 —

Black Harry
in the Paradigm of
"Black Evangelical Identity"

The heritage of ole Black Harry is an exemplary Evangelical model, particularly for African-American Evangelical scholars, leaders, and for the wider Christian community. Students of an Evangelical persuasion may draw significant and livable insights from his life and ministry. To guide these applications, I now turn to "Black Evangelical Identity," the paradigm definition of the group as it appears in *Pro-Black, Pro-Christ, Pro-Cross*.[23]

The paradigm definition projects a biblical image of the African-American Evangelical group, a racially inclusive collective whose core is African-descended. It models Black Evangelicals in a community of culture and theological beliefs. It advocates for developing a positive identity of the group, one that substantively defines them beyond their essential identifying characteristic: black ethno-color. The statement of meaning is descriptive, ascriptive, and prescriptive of the Black Evangelical group. It defines the group's essence, distinctive value, and collective destiny.

As a comprehensive approach, the full text of the paradigm definition "Black Evangelical Identity" spans six pages in its publication.[24]

Several excerpts of the model are useful for highlighting aspects of Black Harry's identity, and facilitate bridging the historical conversation on his life and ministry to contemporary applications. Here we consider the opening paragraph of the identity paradigm.

> Black Evangelicals, at the core of their collective group or gathering, are a Cross-centered community of spiritually impassioned African-descended Gospelizers—"Good News messengers" of their resurrected Lord, Jesus Christ—whose intentionally biblical beliefs and culturally Black way of life both centers them and empowers them to share in His holistic redemptive Cross-bearing experience and mission.[25]

Aspects of the "Black Evangelical Identity" model allow us to illuminate several lessons drawn from the experience and beliefs of Black Harry. Initially, two lessons relate to Black Harry as a Gospelizer and to his racial-ethnic identity. Subsequently, four lessons relate the message and ministry of Black Harry to core beliefs of Black Evangelical faith in the areas of prophesying, *koinonia*-izing, kindred-loving the Black group in racial diversity, and Cross-bearing in redemptive mission.

— 4 —

Black Harry—
A Gospelizer of
African-Descended Distinction

Lesson 1
- **Black Harry—Gospelizer**

A "Gospelizer" is a holistic "Good News messenger" of the resurrected Lord, Jesus Christ. The unique name expresses a holistic concept. "Gospelizer" derives from a New Testament word-group (*Euangelizo/Euangelistes*) covering gracious words, good works, and great workings of God demonstrated by the proactive community of believers spreading the Gospel in its full dimensions.[26]

A careful study of *euangelizo* and *euangelistes* substantiates the following: The verb may be translated as "gospelizing," "bringing the Good News;" and the noun as "gospelizers," "Good News messengers." The Gospel (*euangellion*, "Good News" of Christ), is the root of these terms. When persons identify themselves as "Evangelical," they thereby identify themselves as "messengers of Good News;" even as "angels (*angellos*) of Good News" ("*eu*" = "good"; "*angellos*" = "angel/messenger").[27]

Indeed, *Euangelizo/Euangelistes,* and the activity of Christ's followers these terms describe, connote the idea of holism.

Christian ministry encompasses "Good News" (or Gospel) in **both message and ministry**. Further, the gospelizing ministry encompasses both **good works and miraculous workings**; and, believers perform their gospelizing ministry **personally and collectively**. Their message and ministry influences the public sector with prophetic discourse, social justice, and the like.[28]

Gospelizing, as biblically understood, manifests "great" or miraculous workings. Divine signs and wonders accompany the divine word of Good News. The gospelizing of Black Harry demonstrated these spiritual workings of God. Contemporaries of Black Harry testified to how God used the messenger in the revival services. Bishop Coke wrote of Black Harry, "an amazing power attends his word." Bishop Garrettson wrote, "a general weeping ran through the assembly [at a town in the area of Hudson, N.Y.], especially while Harry gave an exhortation."[29]

Indisputably, the steady rise of Black Harry in popularity as a Gospel preacher leaves little room for debate. God greatly used the illiterate preacher, by setting His servant on a hill to shine the light of Christ all around. Following the time when he entered the ministry as a local preacher or exhorter, the record of Black Harry's contemporaries clearly notes his ever-increasing effectiveness and influence in gospelizing. The following points capture the escalating fashion of his ministry:

1) Initially, Black Harry—essentially functioning in the role of a servant and driver to a bishop—was an exhorter; following the bishop's sermon, he spoke words

encouraging the hearers to heed God's Word.

2) Perceiving the effectiveness of Black Harry, the bishop—using a tag-team approach—assigned Black Harry to preach to the Blacks after the bishop first preached to the whites.

3) Black Harry preached both to the Blacks and the whites who lingered to hear him even after first hearing the bishop's sermon.

4) The bishop announced Black Harry as a headliner preacher to draw more people, Blacks and whites, to the revival meetings.

5) Black Harry preached as a substitute for the bishop in times of his sickness or other matters needing his attention.

6) Black Harry preached to whites who desired to hear him more than they desired to hear the bishop.

Certainly, Black Harry was a "Gospelizer," and in an authentic sense became "all things to all men to save some" (cf. 1 Corinthians 9:22-23). In particular, Black Harry gospelized Blacks, increasingly gospelized mixed audiences, and most effectively gospelized whites, who apparently became his primary audience.[30] Unquestionably, he won souls to Christ by preaching the Good News of salvation from sin and reconciliation with God through the Lord Jesus. Moreover, his message covertly pushed the social envelope against slavery, especially in his ministry alongside Freeborn Garrettson, the outspoken emancipationist.[31] The ministry of Black Harry evinced a fast connection of the spiritual, personal, social, and systemic dimensions of salvation through the Name of Jesus (cf. Acts 4:12; Acts 2:40). The God of Black Harry Who saves the soul, also saves the whole. This is "Good News" indeed.

Lesson 2

• Black Harry—The Black African Wonder

A major constituent of African-descended peoples is dark color, and sometimes extremely dark color. The color of physical African-ness in a given people such as African-Americans may range along the color spectrum from appearing white, to yellow, beige, brown, and black. Certain persons with African-descended ancestors, who may also pass for white, are at one end of the ethno-color spectrum; others of African descent, whose skin tone may approximate black color in its concrete form, are at the other end of the spectrum.

To his contemporaries, Black Harry received distinction as an "African of the Africans,"[32] and as "the African Wonder."[33] A physical description of the preacher portrays him as "*...slim, but very strongly built, and very black.*"[34] A painting based on an engraving reinforces the portrayal of his very dark complexion.[35]

Using biblical language, we may call a person or people whose color is very dark "Kedar," or, translated, "extremely black." The Shulamite of Song of Solomon 1:5 affirmed herself as "black and beautiful" as the "tents of Kedar." Apparently, Black Harry was also "Kedar." In physical complexion, we could identify this distinguished Gospelizer as "midnight black." Contemporaries of Hoosier identified him as "the black," or by the popular designation "Black Harry"[36]—a designation he apparently accepted readily. Therefore, our use of the handle "Black Harry" is not anachronistic, but simply follows the lead of Black Harry's contemporaries and his own acceptance of the personal moniker.

When the contemporaries of Hoosier called him "the black," and we call him "Black Harry," the handle of identification speaks to his racial-ethnic identity, and contextualizes and distinguishes him as a man and minister among his colleagues. Recall a similar use by the early Church at Antioch who, from among their prophets and teachers, distinctly identified a "Simeon called Niger," that is, "Simeon the black man" (see Acts 13:1ff.). "The African Wonder" Harry Hoosier perhaps was a "jet black" wonder to behold, as he passionately preached the Gospel of God's salvation and shined with high quality as a "black light" for Christ.

Use of the appellation "Black Harry" stands in stark contrast to the thinking of some believers who downplay color and racial-cultural characteristics. They hasten into the refuge of a so-called post-racial American society, earmarked by the presidency of African-descended Barack H. Obama. Some believers evangelically identify themselves in a manner contributing toward downplaying the African continent, race, ancient historical heritage, culture, and color of American blacks. They minimize their own blackness. They content themselves with pursuing a so-called "colorless" or "colorblind" Christian faith—notwithstanding their attempts to promote "reconciliation," or the "diversity" of "multiculturalism."[37]

In contrast, a number of Black Evangelicals take the position that dark ethno-color is the starting point when defining African-descended identity. We belong to a pushback remnant seeking to define Black Evangelicals (as distinguished from our white counterparts) by more than simply locating and specifying black identity at a different area of the skin tone color spectrum. As definers of Evangelical Black identity, we see and regard color—along with physical characteristic, culture, and cultural-social consciousness—as four essential constituents of the black identity of African-descended people. Though not equally shared by each individual African-descended person, these racial-ethnic identifiers of the Black group demand basic acceptance.

Some of our Evangelical kindred—either in the flesh or in the Lord—get unsettled when we raise challenging issues related to identity in social, cultural, and especially theological realms. They prickle when confronted with penetrating arguments describing a beyond-the-face identification of African-American Evangelicals— especially when we define the human and ethno-cultural element beyond the distinction of so-called "mere skin color."

Our contention in this area arises from the conviction of a divine call for Black Evangelicals to distinguish and vindicate their racial-ethnic, cultural, and theological identity. Doing so, we are capable of being **pro-Black** *and* **pro-Christ**, without necessarily being anti-white—or necessarily being anti- any color and racial-ethnic characteristic of God-created and valued humanity.[38]

— 5 —

Black Harry and
Core Beliefs of
Black Evangelical Faith

The paradigm definition "Black Evangelical Identity" explains eight core, indispensable, and intentional beliefs. Black Evangelicals adhere to these crucial, Cross-centered doctrines.[39]

First –	**Glorying in the Cross**
Second –	**Becoming "Born Again" by God's Spirit**
Third –	**Exalting the Lord Jesus Christ**
Fourth –	**Consecrating Scripture**
Fifth –	***Koinonia*-izing Believers**
Sixth –	**Loving Our Own Kindred People Naturally**
Seventh –	**Gospelizing the Poor**
Eighth –	**Prophesying in the Name of Jesus Christ**

We can now relate four of the eight crucial beliefs to the experience of Black Harry: prophesying, *koinonia*-izing, kindred-loving the Black group in diversity, and Cross-bearing.

Lesson 3

- **Black Harry and Prophesying**

Black Harry preached hundreds of sermons. His sermon of note is on the parable of "The Barren Fig Tree," Luke 13:6-9. Historians find no exact record of the actual words spoken by Black Harry when he delivered the sermon in May of 1781 at Adams Chapel, Fairfax County, Virginia.[40]

Let us hear the parable of the barren fig tree in the words of Jesus, as recorded in the Gospel of Luke 13:6-9 (NIV):

> [6] Then he told this parable: "A man had a fig tree, planted in his vineyard, and he went to look for fruit on it, but did not find any. [7] So he said to the man who took care of the vineyard, 'For three years now I've been coming to look for fruit on this fig tree and haven't found any. Cut it down! Why should it use up the soil?' [8] "'Sir,' the man replied, 'leave it alone for one more year, and I'll dig around it and fertilize it. [9] If it bears fruit next year, fine! If not, then cut it down.'"

In the fig tree parable, we clearly see the element of mercy as the vineyard caretaker seeks to spare the barren and soil-wasting fig tree from destruction in its fourth year. The patience of divine mercy seemingly would have been a point stressed by the evangelist Black Harry. The text however leaves dangling the final decision made by the vineyard owner on the ultimate fate of the barren fig tree. A prophetic tone is inherent in this point of exposition.

Whether the vineyard owner agreed to heed his caretaker's assessment, or chose to do otherwise, is an open question of interpretation. Should the tree have been (or was the tree in fact) cut down immediately? Alternatively, did the owner show his mercy by extending another year and chance for the barren fig tree to become fruitful? How Black Harry in his exhortations would have understood and explained the parable on these points is an open question. In contrast, fewer questions would have remained unanswered about a point stressing the divine requirement of believers to become fruitful or to risk the obvious judgment of God. Herein lies the prophetic emphasis of Black Harry.

Using as a point of departure Black Harry's sermon motif of the barren fig tree, travel with me from Jesus' parable of the barren fig tree to the actual practice of the Lord when dealing with one. To our benefit, the Gospels record Jesus' actual historical experience in dealing with a barren fig tree as He approached the time of His Passion at Jerusalem. Fortunately, the biblical text leaves no room for speculating about the outcome.

Both *Matthew* (21:18-22) and *Mark* record the experience of Jesus with the barren fig tree. *Mark's* record of the incident appears in chapter 11, verses 11-14 and 20-25. The *New International Version* reads this way:

> [11] Jesus entered Jerusalem and went to the temple. He looked around at everything, but since it was already late, he went out to Bethany with the Twelve. [12] The next day as they were leaving Bethany, Jesus was hungry. [13] Seeing in the distance a fig tree in leaf, he went to find out if it had any fruit. When he reached it, he found nothing but leaves, because it was not the season for figs. [14] Then he said to the tree, "May no one ever eat fruit from you again." And his disciples heard him say it....[20] In the morning, as they went along, they saw the fig tree withered

from the roots. [21] Peter remembered and said to Jesus, "Rabbi, look! The fig tree you cursed has withered!" [22] "Have[a] faith in God," Jesus answered. [23] "I tell you the truth, if anyone says to this mountain, 'Go, throw yourself into the sea,' and does not doubt in his heart but believes that what he says will happen, it will be done for him. [24] Therefore I tell you, whatever you ask for in prayer, believe that you have received it, and it will be yours. [25] And when you stand praying, if you hold anything against anyone, forgive him, so that your Father in heaven may forgive you your sins.[b]"

The Gospel accounts of Jesus' encounter with the barren fig tree are prophetic. One day, Jesus curses the barren fig tree to be forever fruitless, and the next morning the tree is completely withered (vv. 14 and 20). The Gospel of *Mark* positions the fig-tree account alongside several events: 1) Jesus' Triumphal Entry into Jerusalem, 2) His cleansing of the temple, and 3) questions by His detractors on the source of His authority. This order adds significance to the prophetic tone of the fig-tree event.[41] Moreover, Jesus exhorts the disciples to apply His teaching by praying and faith-speaking to mountains blocking their way, casting them into the sea (11:20-26). This application further enhances the prophetic lesson of the barren fig tree.

By genuinely explaining the essential meaning of the text, the content of Black Harry's preaching on the barren fig tree would bespeak a prophetic theological posture. The analysis holds true whether the exhortations of Black Harry stayed with Jesus' parable

---

[a] Some early manuscripts *If you have*
[b] Some manuscripts *sins. But if you do not forgive, neither will your Father who is in heaven forgive your sins.*

or creatively bridged his message to the Savior's practice. Black Harry's Gospel message implicitly engaged the major social, racial, and economic issues of his day: **racial prejudice, slavery,** and **its abolition.** Inherently, his theology addressed the issues of **freedom, equality,** and **empowerment** of African-descended people in their entirety. Black Harry's message was prophetic gospelizing, and his call to repentance, forgiveness and salvation would have certainly pricked the hearts of those who supported racial prejudice and the system of slavery.

Thus, the Gospel message of Black Harry would have connected evangelism and social justice in a time of systemic change. Eliminating the mountain of slavery and establishing legal and social freedom would have been the strong conviction, albeit covert exhortation, of Black Harry. His fig tree sermon would have placed the church on notice: **God's salvation demands personal and racial fruitfulness.** Perhaps Black Harry inferred (or predicted) in his message that some supposed "saints" faced the judgment of God for failure to oppose slavery or racial inequality. Mercy was available for sinners for a while, but divine judgment was imminent for unrepentant, fruitless sinners.[42] Black Harry's biblical message of the barren fig tree would seem to align perfectly with adopting such a socially prophetic theological position. This is especially the case when Black Harry theologically dared to challenge the divine election and perseverance of professing believers.[43]

Lesson 4

- **Black Harry and *Koinonia*-izing**

Black Harry found himself living and doing ministry with a theology betwixt the kingdom of God and the *Koinonia*. He submitted to preaching the Gospel of the Lord's authority and kingdom. Yet, he found himself amidst a church denying him full participation in *Koinonia*, the Cross-bearing fellowship-community of the Church. Based on race, the Methodist church did not allow either Black Harry or Richard Allen to have a role at the Christmas Conference in 1784 (the meeting that officially organized American Methodism); the two preachers were non-voting representatives. Further, though received as a preacher, Black Harry never received ordination as a deacon or elder of the church.[44] Webb states,

> Unlike Allen, Hoosier chose to accept his subordinate role in a Methodist church that was dominated by a white leadership. Hoosier seemed resigned that his popularity did not lead to more recognition or respect. At least publicly he was able to accept the tensions of being both a servant and a preacher, but privately he must have suffered many humiliations.[45]

The story of Black Harry's encounter with a white host—who declared, "she would not hear the black"—highlights his struggle for *Koinonia*.[46] Overhearing the remark, Black Harry responded by praying that afternoon. Later in the service, after the message by a "brother W.," Black Harry humbly spoke of how all people suffer from sin, but God sent a remedy by a physician to heal sinners from their condition—a physician who was Black! Sinners faced the possibility, however, that some might reject God's messenger and physician because his hands were black.

Black Harry continued his exhortation, touching the hearts of everyone present. Afterward, Black Harry gave a powerful prayer. That night, God used the words and prayers of Black Harry to convict his host and a number of other gatherers of their racial prejudice. They were "cut to the heart," responded to the Gospel, and changed their prejudicial ways.[47]

Black Harry's evangelistic message covered forgiveness of sin, and repentance from racial prejudice or ethno-centrism. In his message, we see the spiritual seeds of racial reconciliation in the Gospel. We see the *Koinonia* of God in the Gospel of salvation.

Derived from a study of the N.T. word *koinonia*, and the concepts it connotes in various references to believers, I offer the following expanded definition of the concept:

> "*Koinonia*" is the common and shared relational experience of believers with the Father and His Son in the union, communion, unity, resources, partnership, fellowship, and community of the people of God that the Holy Spirit creates in the Church.[48]

The biblical teaching of "the *Koinonia*"[49]—as God's true, sacred, and reconciled community for His people—"has far-reaching ramifications for the way the people of God do Church. It informs our theological thinking and practices in the area of structuring the interrelationships of believers. Furthermore, the *Koinonia* certainly challenges, or disallows the following:"[50]

> Restricting the full exercise of God's spiritual gifts in the Body, or limiting their expression to only certain persons or groups, rather than encouraging mutual gift sharing in the freedom

of the Spirit;....[It also prohibits] age, class, ethno-cultural, or racial characteristics that some use as barriers to impede or prevent full communal participation and empowerment.[51]

Lesson 5

- **Black Harry and Kindred-Loving the Black Group in Racial Diversity**

I have identified "Loving Our Own Kindred People Naturally" as the sixth core belief of Black Evangelical faith.[52]

> Love of the Black self and for the Black group—as the first-fruit manifestation of love for all of God's humanity—are essential theological beliefs of those who identify themselves as African-descended Evangelicals.[53]

The primary basis for this belief are the words of Jesus who said, "Thou shalt love thy neighbour as thyself" (Matthew 22:39; Mark 12:31). Additional arguments are based on the biblical love concept of *storgos*—"**love of kindred, especially of parents for children and children for parents**"—which establish a righteous Black self-love of the group.[54]

How the church treated Black Harry impacts ways of thinking about group Black self-love and Evangelical racial diversity. Black Evangelicals grapple with issues of identity and community amidst Evangelical ideas of racial diversity and multi-culturalism. "The Cultural Diversity," chapter 11 of *Pro-Black, Pro-Christ, Pro-Cross,* deals with "evangelically empowering Black peoplehood in inter-racial and cross-cultural relations, and in reconciliation." I gear this teaching essentially toward helping Black people to love their own in the midst of a growing multi-culturalism. With this aim at heart, I state 15 values, principles, and statements of cultural diversity. Identity and *koinonia* are two of the 15 values pertaining to the present discussion.

The first principle is on identity in diversity. Christ-centered, ethno-cultural diversity requires "identity in diversity without **assimilated ethnicity.**" "Diversity, in its spirit or practice, should not cause those who participate in this movement to lose, devalue, or denigrate their personal or ethno-cultural identity and beauty in the group context."[55]

Koinonia in diversity (the seventh of 15 principles) applies to how the church treated Black Harry, and influences our ways of thinking in this area. Christ-centered diversity requires *"**koinonia in diversity** without classified community."* "Attaining the spiritual union and communion of *koinonia* in diversity is an imperative value of Christian community, whose members must never operate their fellowship in the destructive spirit of class-driven stratifying, or in an impersonal or detached manner."[56]

Self-love for the Black group supports African-descended identity and *koinonia* in a context of diversity.

Lesson 6

- **Black Harry and Cross-bearing**

Finally, the life of Black Harry evinces the belief and spirit of Cross-bearing. The Black Evangelical paradigm states that African-descended believers ascribe to a definition centering and empowering them to share in the "**holistic redemptive Cross-bearing experience and mission**" of Christ.[57]

In his ministry, Black Harry appears to have borne a cross. Consider the emotional and spiritual trouble he most certainly experienced. On the one hand, he was one of the greatest preachers of his day; on the other hand, the Methodist church relegated him to second-class status.[58] Black Harry's evangelistic powers saved thousands. Concurrently, his lack of ecclesiastical empowerment prohibited him from fully discipling the converts he won. The church used Black Harry to win souls and organize believers,[59] but refused him the rite of ordination as a Methodist deacon or elder, and thus denied him the full rights and powers to shepherd converted souls on their spiritual journey.

As Black Harry labored under such spiritually and racially discordant circumstances, one can only imagine that on numerous occasions he would have contemplated walking away from the church's ecclesiastical hypocrisy. When Richard Allen, his contemporary, faced similar racism and prejudice, he chose to take an alternate course and empowered himself. The historical result and fruit is the African Methodist Episcopal Church, organized in 1816.[60]

Yet, Black Harry settled himself to live with a very awkward ministerial arrangement within the church and persevered in the Gospel ministry. He endured the disrespect and lack of honor that all genuine prophets seemingly must endure from time to time. Enduring so, Black Harry continued gospelizing tirelessly and sacrificially,[61] winning converts to the Lord and members to the church, even while despising the shame of ecclesiastical racism and accepting a crucifixion of sorts (cf. Hebrews 12:1-2). Black Harry fixed his eyes on Jesus, and on "the joy that lay before" him, and thus enabled himself to carry a burdensome and vexing Cross.

While reviewing Evangelical definitions of African-American adherents, I discovered an article by Reverend Dr. William Hiram Bentley, the highly respected "Father" of the National Black Evangelical Association. He defined four principles and resulting action-responses of Black Evangelicalism. I state the fourth and final principle of this "certified Black Evangelical," to use his own phrase. Bentley writes,

> Finally, (and this is the penetrating principle), the ruling predisposition of it all, from start to finish—the interpenetration at every level, and at all times, consciously and unconsciously, with the determination to make all things obedient to the will of Christ as revealed in God's Word, and most clearly in the demands of the Gospel of our Lord Jesus Christ. As it is said of Christ, that as He surrenders up the Messianic kingdom to His Father, "that God may be all in all," even so will we at any time, and all times, surrender up, with joyous devotion and adoration, our peculiar priorities, so that at all times Christ may be all in all.[62]

I believe Black Harry submitted to the ruling predisposition of obedience to the will of Christ, and that he surrendered, with joyous devotion and adoration **his peculiar priorities**, so that at all times in his life (or in the greater part of his sojourn) Christ became all in all. Following in the footsteps of Christ Jesus, Black Harry humbled himself and bore the Cross of suffering and redemption. Black Harry lived the Word. He honored Christ by bearing the Cross in his missional formation to the glory of God. Parenthetically, I believe Richard Allen too bore the Cross. He took a course that God required of him, albeit in a way differing from the requirements of God's cross for Black Harry. Whether of Allen, Black Harry, or ourselves, the cross that Jesus requires of His followers on a daily basis is quite personal, and uncomfortably public.

Black Harry shouldered the Cross of ecclesiastical indignity and disrespect, and faithfully continued in God's will and grace. Though his life suffered backsliding—a major spiritual setback—Black Harry prayed his way through, ultimately recovered, and received restoration. The words of a hymn by Lucy C. Campbell capture the Cross-bearing experience of the Black African Wonder, Harry Hoosier. The hymn is "He'll Understand, and Say 'Well done'." Consider the fourth verse:

> *But if you try and fail in your trying,*
> > *hands sore and scarred from the work you've begun;*
> *Take up your cross, run quickly to meet Him;*
> > *He'll understand, He'll say, "Well done."*
> Refrain:
> > *Oh when I come to the end of my journey,*
> > > *Weary of life and the battle is won;*
> > *Carrying the staff and the cross of redemption,*
> > > *He'll understand and say "Well done."* [63]

We believe the gracious Lord has said, "Well done" to ole Black Harry, the African-descended Gospelizer.

— 6 —

Black Harry and Unfinished Church Business

Several calls to action are in order to finish the church business of ole Black Harry. First, the church should authorize and sanction a complete official biography of Black Harry. A person of African descent should write the manuscript, perhaps assisted by a white believer. The life of Black Harry deserves nothing less than our capturing it in a codified document.

Second, on occasion, a sector of society acknowledges and awards a person posthumously, seeking to rectify the group's blatant mistakes and moral oversight, and to right historical injustices. In this vein, I ask: Would it not be righteous for the collective church bodies of Methodism to confer posthumously upon Black Harry a well-deserved ordination into the deaconate and eldership of the Methodist church, as was petitioned by a group of conscientious Methodist preachers in 1805?[64]

Such a courageous, repentant, and prophetic action by the church would signal a genuine move toward racial restitution and reconciliation within Evangelical circles of the Christian faith. Honoring Black Harry in the fashion of an ordination might also inspire countless African-descended and other Evangelicals worldwide to emulate the worthy model of this historic witness of the Lord Jesus Christ.

Herein, as president of the National Black Evangelical Association and a member of the Obsidian Society—and trusting that others of good conscience will join me—I make this call for the posthumous ecclesiastical ordination of Black Harry Hoosier—a formally uneducated but highly exemplary Black Evangelical minister of great faith, dedication, and sacrifice—an African-descended Gospelizer par excellence in his generation. [65]

Monday, February 4 in the year of our LORD *2013*

# # #

Endnotes

[1] The present publication revises and expands an original paper presented for The Obsidian Society, at its February 3 – 4, 2013 meeting at Asbury Theological Seminary in Orlando, FL. Obsidian held its meeting in conjunction with Asbury's dedication of the Harry Hosier Institute. The theme of the historic gathering was "Embracing the Kingdom: Living the Call in Times of Change." The original presentation was titled, "African-descended Gospelizer Black Harry: Harry Hoosier & Living Out the Word of God."

[2] Chicago: Black Light Fellowship, 2012.

[3] See Richardson, *Dark Salvation,* 171, cited below.

Information I present on the life of Black Harry draws upon mostly secondary sources, their references, and general sources, and accessed via the Internet:

Richardson, Harry Van Buren. *Dark Salvation: The Story of Methodism as it Developed Among Blacks in America (*C. Eric Lincoln Series on Black Religion). Garden City, NY: Anchor Press/Doubleday, 1976.

Webb, Stephen H. "Introducing Black Harry Hoosier: The History Behind Indiana's Namesake," *Indiana Magazine of History*, XCVIII (March 2002), Trustees of Indiana University; "The Origin of the Word 'Hoosier': A New Interpretation," *Indiana Magazine of History*, XCI (June 1995), 189-96.

Webb builds upon the work of Piersen, William D., "The Origin of the Word 'Hoosier': A New Interpretation," *Indiana Magazine* of *History,* XCI (June 1995), 189-96.

Smith, Warren Thomas. *Harry Hoosier: Circuit Rider.* Nashville: Upper Room Books, 1981. A bibliography of "Black Harry," a Methodist circuit preacher par excellence in the colonial period.

Webber, R. (1994). *Vol. 2: Twenty Centuries of Christian Worship.* The Complete Library of Christian Worship (104). Nashville: Star Song Publishing Group.

Raybold, Rev. G. A., *Reminiscences of Methodism in West Jersey.* New York: Lane & Scott, 1849.

McEllhenney, John G. "Harry Hosier: An African American Who Gave a Beat to Methodist Preaching c. 1750-c.1806," http://nccumc.org/history/memorable-methodist/harry-hosier/ (accessed 12/31/2012).

Morgan, Philip D., *Slave Counterpoint: Black Culture in the Eighteenth-Century Chesapeake & Lowcountry.* Chapel Hill: University of North Carolina Press, 1998.

Barton, David. "God: Missing in Action from American History," *The NRB Magazine,* 2005. http://www.freerepublic.com/focus/f-news/1468215/posts (accessed 12/31/2012).

Graf, Jeffery, "The Word *Hoosier.*" Reference Department, Herman B. Wells Library, Indiana University-Bloomington. http://www.indiana.edu/~librcsd/internet/extra/hoosier.html (accessed 12/31/2012).

"The Rev. 'Black Harry' Hoosier (or Hosier) 1750-1810," *Honoring Godly Heroes: African American History Month. The Wallbuilder Report,* 2005.

Jenkins, Jeff. "The Rev. 'Black Harry' Hoosier (or Hosier) 1750-1810," *Thoughts and Theology,* May 14, 2009. http://jeffjenkinsocala.blogspot.com/2009/05/rev-black-harry-hoosier-or-hosier-1750.html (accessed 12/31/2012).

"Harry Hoosier," WFIU Staff, October 4, 2004. http://indianapublicmedia.org/momentofindianahistory/harry-hoosier/ (accessed 12/31/2012).

[4] Piersen, William D. "Origin of the Word 'Hoosier.'" Since Black Harry could not read or write, no record exists of how he would have chosen to spell his own name. Various spellings and renderings of his name include: Hosier, Hoosier, Hoshur, and Hossier, as well as

Henry Hoshur, Harry Hoshur, Hanry Hoshure, Black Harvey, Henry Hersure, and Henry Hosure. For simplicity, I've chosen "Hoosier" as the name to use in this publication. See Graf, "The Word *Hoosier*," who cites Warren Thomas Smith, *Harry Hosier: Circuit Rider*, and the unpublished journal of William Colbert (1764-1835).

[5] Webb, "Introducing Black Harry," 34, on Hoosier's relationship to Harry Dorsey Gough (17??-1808); and McEllhenney, "Harry Hosier: A Beat to Methodist Preaching."

[6] See the testimonies of Black Harry's effectiveness, cited by Morgan, *Slave Counterpoint*, 655. Apparently, Black Harry's preaching ability existed in disproportion to his reading inability. "While Harry was travelling with Bishop Allen, the bishop attempted to teach him to read, (for he could not read;) but, to use Harry's phrase, 'when he tried to read, he lost the gift of preaching,' and so gave it up entirely." Raybold, *Reminiscences*, 166.

[7] Barton, "God: Missing in Action from American History."

[8] Graf, "The Word Hoosier." Webb, "Introducing Black Harry," 30.

[9] Richardson, *Dark Salvation*, 172. In addition, Black Harry is the first Black or white Methodist whose preaching is noted in a New York newspaper, the *Packet* (*Ibid.*, 171). See also, "Honoring Godly Heroes," 6, "...he became famous as a traveling evangelist and was considered one of the most popular preachers of his era."

[10] Webb, "Introducing Black Harry," 41.

[11] Richardson, *Dark Salvation*, 172, records the words of Garrettson on Black Harry's acceptance by non-Methodists, "The different denominations heard him with much admiration..."

[12] Webb, "Introducing Black Harry," 36. Quoting Raybold, *Reminiscences*, 167.

[13] See Garrettson's testimony in Richardson, *Dark Salvation*, 172, "Quakers thought that as he was unlearned he must preach by immediate inspiration."

[14] Webb, "Introducing Black Harry," 39. Quoting Henry Boehm.

[15] *Ibid.,* 33. Richardson, *Dark Salvation*, 171.

[16] *Ibid.,* 36.

[17] *Ibid.,* 38.

[18] "Garrettson traveled widely, and his message of Christian perfection, pacifism and aggressive abolitionism provoked life-threatening opposition as well as imprisonment. Nevertheless, his evangelistic efforts resulted in the founding of new churches in New York. In 1784, when Thomas Coke came with instructions from John Wesley to organize the American Methodist Church, Garrettson summoned ministers to the *Christmas Conference* of 1784." Reid, D. G., Linder, R. D., Shelley, B. L., & Stout, H. S. (1990). *Dictionary of Christianity in America.* Downers Grove, IL: InterVarsity Press.

Webb, "Introducing Black Harry," 37-38, states, "Beginning in 1789, Hoosier traveled with Freeborn Garrettson (1752-1827), a Methodist preacher who upon conversion freed his slaves and became an ardent emancipationist. Garrettson was often criticized for preaching against slavery, and his outspoken views must have put Hoosier in a dangerous position. Their views on grace and free will were even more threatening to many in their audiences. Garrettson and Hoosier were often verbally abused and sometimes physically attacked because they denied the Calvinist doctrines of unconditional election and the perseverance of the saints, which were dominant among Protestants at the time. One of Hoosier's favorite biblical texts was the story of the barren fig tree, which Jesus cursed when he found it had nothing but leaves. Hoosier used this story to illustrate the idea that salvation should lead to good works. If Christians did not show the fruit of their faith by striving to be holy, then they could fall from grace and thus risk being cursed by God."

[19] Webb, "Introducing Black Harry," 40. Black Harry was a licensed exhorter or local preacher. He could have been ordained as a deacon, and subsequently as an elder. In 1805, 19 preachers signed a petition for his ordination at the Methodist bishops' meeting at the

Philadelphia Conference. The church leadership never heeded the call on behalf of Black Harry.

Neither did the church heed the call for the ordination of other African-Americans. See Richardson, *Dark Salvation*, 170. Concerning earliest Black preachers in the Methodist Episcopal Church, "The main reason these men left the Methodist Church was the reluctance of that body to accept them fully into its ministries, especially in the work with blacks, and used them as exhorters and local preachers, the lowest order in the Methodist hierarchy. But despite repeated appeals over a long time, the Church would not ordain them as deacons, the middle rank, and certainly not as elders, the highest rank. It was not until 1800 that the General Conference agreed to ordain even black local deacons."

[20] Webb, "Introducing Black Harry," 40.

[21] Richardson, *Dark Salvation*, 173-174. Quoting Abel Stevens, a Methodist historian: "Self-abased and contrite, [Black Harry] started one evening down the Neck, below Southwark, Philadelphia, determined to remain till his backslidings were healed. Under a tree he wrestled in prayer into the watches of the night. Before the morning God restored him to the joys of his salvation. Thenceforward he continued faithful. He resumed his public labors, and about the year [1806] died in Philadelphia, 'making a good end,' and was borne to the grave by a great procession of both white and black admirers, who buried him as a hero, once overcome, but finally victorious." See also "Honoring Godly Heroes," 8.

[22] Raybold cites Black Harry's description of the "Elocution of Faith," *Reminiscences,* 166-67. Webb, "Introducing Black Harry," 36. Richardson, *Dark Salvation,* 181.

[23] McCray, *Pro-Black, Pro-Christ, Pro-Cross,* chapter 5, "The Crafted Paradigm-Definition."

[24] *Ibid.,* 53-60

[25] *Ibid.,* 53.

[26] McCray, *Gospelizers! Terrorized and Intensified,* 46ff., 54ff. Black Light Fellowship, 2002.

[27] McCray, *Pro-Black, Pro-Christ, Pro-Cross,* 80.

[28] *Ibid.,* 79-81.

[29] Richardson, *Dark Salvation,* 172, 173.

[30] Morgan, *Slave Counterpoint,* 430, 655. "Some black evangelicals influenced whites even more directly: they preached to them. The most famous black preacher was 'Black Harry,' or Harry Hoosier, who often rode with Francis Asbury."

[31] Understandably, places outside the South—an area especially fraught with dangers for an outspoken ex-slave—would best receive Black Harry's message of emancipation. "Harry seems never to have traveled into the heart of the slaveholding South." *Ibid.,* 655.

[32] McEllhenney, "Harry Hoosier: A Beat to Methodist Preaching," quoting Henry Boehm: "He [Black Harry] was very black, an African of the Africans."

[33] "...Jeffrey Bewley, a coloured preacher, and himself a wonder for capacity and performances, in eulogizing Black Harry, applied a term by which he was well known: 'Herein lies the African wonder'." Raybold, *Reminiscences,* 168.

[34] Webb, "Introducing Black Harry," 35, quoting G. A. Raybold, *Reminiscences of Methodism in West Jersey* (New York, 1849), 166-67.

[35] The painting is by Thomas Coke Ruckle. See Webb, "Introducing Black Harry," 31-32.

[36] Richardson, *Dark Salvation,* 171.

[37] Perhaps Black Evangelicals downplay the virtues of their group for reasons related to their desires for white believers to accept them, for "oneness," or for financial support of their ministries. Motives are varied. Cf. Allen's statement, "Many resolute observers also doubt the independence of Black Evangelicals who uncritically adopt the conventions of their simplistic mentors in order to attract funding or media sponsorship. Truth always matters. Hypocrisy always stinks,

in and out of the academy or church!" "What Is a Black Evangelical? What Do They Do?: Fresh Definitions and Future Strategies," 7, 2006. The deficiencies of white American Evangelicalism increasingly constrain Black Evangelical adherents and scholarship to adopt a posture that insists on recognizing and accepting genuine, beyond-the-color, definition of the Black Evangelical. Sechrest comments, "Universalism in Christianity has invariably constructed identity around a White male ideal, and color blindness, sadly, often results in more losses than gains for African Americans in society...Instead, the gift that African Americans bring to the community of the redeemed is an awareness of how race shapes our identity as Christians." "Who Is My Brother," 46ff. *Journal of African American Christian Thought*, 2009.

[38] McCray, *Pro-Black, Pro-Christ, Pro-Cross,* 76.

[39] *Ibid.,* 220-300, "The Core Theology" (chapter 15) biblically exposits "eight indispensable tenets of Black Evangelical faith."

[40] "Black Harry Hoosier: Orator of Spirit," in the *African American Registry*. http://www.aaregistry.org/historic_events/view/black-harry-hosier-orator-spirit (accessed 2/8/2013).

[41] 11:1-11, The Triumphal Entry; 11:12-14, Cursing of the Fig Tree; 11:15-19, Cleansing of the Temple; 11:20-26, Lesson of the Withered Fig Tree; 11:27-33, Source of Jesus' Authority.

[42] See note 18 above. "Hoosier used this story to illustrate the idea that salvation should lead to good works. If Christians did not show the fruit of their faith by striving to be holy, then they could fall from grace and thus risk being cursed by God." Webb, "Introducing Black Harry," 38.

[43] See the comment of Asbury about Hoosier, in Richardson, *Dark Salvation,* 173, "...certain sectarians are greatly displeased with him, because he tells them they may fall from grace, and that they must be holy."

[44] Webb, "Introducing Black Harry," 40.

[45] *Ibid.,* 39.

[46] Raybold, *Reminiscences,* 167.

[47] *Ibid.,* 167. Webb, "Introducing Black Harry," 36-37.

[48] McCray, *Pro-Black, Pro-Christ, Pro-Cross,* 288, note 74.

[49] Acts 2:42, "They devoted themselves to the apostles' teaching and to **the fellowship,** to the breaking of bread and to prayer" (emphasis added). See the discussion on the *Koinonia* in McCray, *Pro-Black, Pro-Christ, Pro-Cross,* 250ff.

[50] *Ibid.,* 253.

[51] *Ibid.,* 253.

[52] *Ibid.,* 282.

[53] *Ibid.,* 261.

[54] *Ibid.,* 256-257.

[55] *Ibid.,* 154.

[56] Bishop Freeborn Garrettson did not use the title "brother" when referring to Black Harry, as he would refer to other preachers. That is to say, he never called the exhorter "Brother Harry," but simply "Harry." See McEllhenney, "Harry Hoosier: A Beat to Methodist Preaching."

[57] McCray, *Pro-Black, Pro-Christ, Pro-Cross,* 53. Sometimes "Cross" is capitalized either to indicate the unique atoning death of Christ at Calvary, or to highlight the spiritual nature of the suffering that believers experience in their close relation with the Redeemer. A believer's suffering is often much more than a social experience.

[58] At the February 2013 Obsidian meeting, Dr. Carolyn Gordon gave an excellent presentation on Black Harry, stressing why he might have made "The Barren Fig Tree" his sermon of choice. She clearly analyzed the social situation of the ex-slave Black Harry: "Manumission in some areas left a cloud of possible re-enslavement and suspect" hanging over his head. In his itinerant ministry with the church, the revivalist lived in two worlds: "the less than and the more than." He was "bi-formed: almost, but not yet."

[59] Richardson, *Dark Salvation,* 170-171.

[60] Richard Allen and Daniel Coker organized the denomination. Allen

became the first Black Bishop in Protestantism. See Richardson, *Dark Salvation*, 174.

[61] Richardson, *Dark Salvation*, 37.

[62] Bentley, *Understanding the History of NBEA*, 2. National Black Evangelical Association, Chicago, IL, 1988. Cf. 1 Corinthians 15:28, "Now when all things are made subject to Him, then the Son Himself will also be subject to Him who put all things under Him, that God may be all in all" (NKJV). The other three Evangelical principles and resulting action-responses Bentley provides deal with reading correctly the national situation of Black Americans, developing a national Black American strategy, and a healthy concept of Black group identity.

[63] "He'll Understand, and Say, 'Well Done,'" fourth stanza, Lucy E. Campbell, (1885-1963).

[64] The call in 2013 for the ordination of Black Harry comes nearly 208 years after the initial call in 1805 by 19 Methodist preachers. See note 19.

[65] The idea to ordain Black Harry posthumously came through interaction with the racially perceptive Attorney Lester L. Barclay of the Chicago firm, The Barclay Law Group. He noted the action taken on February 17, 2012 by the Board of Trustees of the University of Pennsylvania with regard to the late African-American intellectual and social giant William Edward Burghardt "W. E. B." Du Bois (1868-1963). Initiated by Sociology Department Chair Tukufu Zuberi, UPenn posthumously bestowed on Du Bois an honorary emeritus professorship in the departments of Sociology and Africana Studies. Racism was the only reason Du Bois did not receive a professorship when he taught at the university in 1896. Du Bois was a founder of the National Association for the Advancement of Colored People (NAACP) and many recognize him as the father of the Pan-African Movement. http://www.thedp.com/article/2012/02/w.e.b._du_bois_receives_honorary_emeritus_professorship (accessed 2/1/2013).

BLACK LIGHT FELLOWSHIP

"A Beacon of Christ"
P.O. Box 5369
Chicago, IL 60680

773.826.7790

www.blacklightfellowship.com

www.TheAfricanWonderBlackHarryHoosier.com

Email: info@blacklightfellowship.com

BLACK LIGHT FELLOWSHIP

"A Beacon of Christ"
P.O. Box 5369
Chicago, IL 60680

773.826.7790

www.blacklightfellowship.com

www.TheAfricanWonderBlackHarryHoosier.com

Email: info@blacklightfellowship.com